What Is the International Monetary Fund?

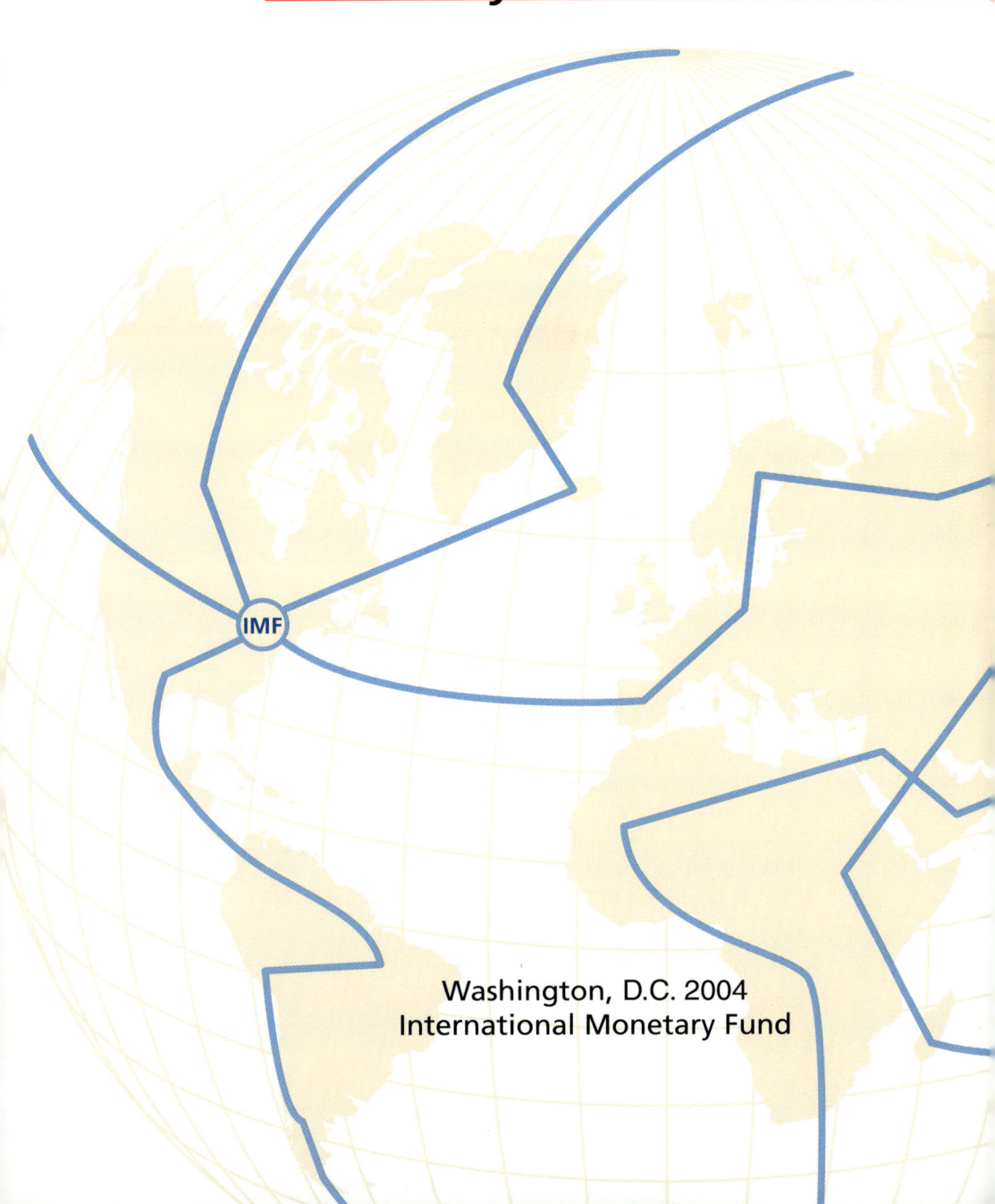

Washington, D.C. 2004
International Monetary Fund

© 2001 International Monetary Fund

Editor
Jeremy Clift

Production: IMF Graphics Section
Cover and design: Luisa Menjivar-Macdonald
Typesetting: Julio R. Prego, Joseph A. Kumar
Revisions: Alicia Etchebarne-Bourdin

ISBN 1-55775-920-0

Published August 2001
Reprinted February 2003
Revised July 2004

To order IMF publications, please contact:
International Monetary Fund, Publication Services
700 19th Street, N.W., Washington, D.C., 20431, U.S.A.
Tel.: (202) 623-7430   Telefax: (202) 623-7201
E-mail: publications@imf.org
Internet: http://www.imf.org

CONTENTS

iv	Preface
2	The IMF's Role at a Glance
6	Adapting to Meet New Challenges
8	The Origins of the IMF
13	Who Makes Decisions at the IMF?
16	Where Does the IMF Get Its Money?
19	How Does the IMF Serve Its Members?
30	Highlights in the Evolution of IMF Lending
34	IMF Technical Assistance and Training
36	Strengthening the International Monetary and Financial System
46	A New Approach to Reducing Poverty in Low-Income Countries

Boxes

5	The IMF's Main Business; Macroeconomic and Financial Sector Policies
11	The IMF's Purposes
18	What Is an SDR?
27	Selected IMF Lending Facilities
50	Formulating Poverty Reduction Strategies

Preface

The International Monetary Fund is frequently in the news, but its role and functions are often misunderstood. This pamphlet aims to explain them.

Further information on the IMF can be obtained from the IMF's website (*www.imf.org*), including the full text of the IMF's *Annual Report*, the biweekly *IMF Survey* and its annual *Supplement on the IMF*, Fact Sheets, pamphlets, and other publications.

This pamphlet was prepared by staff of the IMF's External Relations Department.

The IMF is an organization of 184 countries, working to foster global monetary cooperation, secure financial stability, facilitate international trade, promote high employment and sustainable economic growth, and reduce poverty.

The IMF is governed by its 184 member countries

The International Monetary Fund was established by international treaty in 1945 to help promote the health of the world economy. Headquartered in Washington, D.C., it is governed by its almost global membership of 184 countries.

The IMF is the **central institution** of the international monetary system—the system of international payments and exchange rates among national currencies that enables business to take place between countries.

It aims to **prevent crises** in the system by encouraging countries to adopt sound economic policies; it is also—as its name suggests—**a fund** that can be tapped by members needing temporary financing to address balance of payments problems.

A Global Institution
The IMF's Role at a Glance

The IMF's **statutory purposes** include promoting the balanced expansion of world trade, the stability of exchange rates, the avoidance of competitive currency devaluations, and the orderly correction of a country's balance of payments problems.

To serve these purposes, the IMF:

- **monitors** economic and financial developments and policies, in member countries and at the global level, and gives **policy advice** to its members based on its more than fifty years of experience. For example:

    In its annual review of the Japanese economy for 2003, the IMF Executive Board urged Japan to adopt a comprehensive approach to revitalize the corporate and financial sectors of its economy, tackle deflation, and address fiscal imbalances.

    The IMF commended Mexico in 2003 for good economic management, but said structural reform of the tax system, energy sector, the labor market, and judicial system was needed to help the country compete in the global economy.

    In its Spring 2004 World Economic Outlook, the IMF said an orderly resolution of global imbalances, notably the large U.S. current account deficit and surpluses elsewhere, was needed as the global economy recovered and moved toward higher interest rates.

The IMF works for global prosperity by promoting

- **the balanced expansion of world trade,**
- **stability of exchange rates,**
- **avoidance of competitive devaluations, and**
- **orderly correction of balance of payments problems**

- **lends** to member countries with balance of payments problems, not just to provide temporary financing but to support adjustment and reform policies aimed at correcting the underlying problems. For example:

    During the 1997-98 Asian financial crisis, the IMF acted swiftly to help Korea bolster its reserves. It pledged $21 billion to assist Korea to reform its economy, restructure its financial and corporate sectors, and recover from recession. Within four years, Korea had recovered sufficiently to repay the loans and, at the same time, rebuild its reserves.

    In October 2000, the IMF approved an additional $52 million loan for Kenya to help it cope with the effects of a severe drought, as part of a three-year $193 million loan under the IMF's Poverty Reduction and Growth Facility, a concessional lending program for low-income countries.

- provides the governments and central banks of its member countries with **technical assistance** and training in its areas of expertise. For example:

    Following the collapse of the Soviet Union, the IMF stepped in to help the Baltic states, Russia, and other former Soviet countries set up treasury systems for their central banks as part of the transition from centrally planned to market-based economic systems.

As the only international agency whose mandated activities involve active dialogue with virtually every country on economic policies, the IMF is the principal **forum** for discussing not only national economic policies in a global context, but also issues important to the stability of the international monetary and financial system. These include countries' choice of exchange rate arrangements, the avoidance of destabilizing international capital flows, and the design of internationally recognized standards and codes for policies and institutions.

By working to strengthen the international financial system and to accelerate progress toward reducing poverty, as

Box 1
The IMF's Main Business: Macroeconomic and Financial Sector Policies

In its oversight of member countries' economic policies, the IMF looks mainly at the performance of an economy as a whole—often referred to as its **macroeconomic performance**. This comprises total spending (and its major components like consumer spending and business investment), output, employment, and inflation, as well as the country's balance of payments—that is, the balance of a country's transactions with the rest of the world.

The IMF focuses mainly on a country's **macroeconomic policies**—that is, policies relating to the government's budget, the management of interest rates, money, and credit, and the exchange rate—and **financial sector** policies, including the regulation and supervision of banks and other financial institutions. In addition, the IMF pays due attention to **structural** policies that affect macroeconomic performance—including labor market policies that affect employment and wage behavior. The IMF advises each member on how its policies in these areas may be improved to allow the more effective pursuit of goals such as high employment, low inflation, and sustainable economic growth—that is, growth that can be sustained without leading to such difficulties as inflation and balance of payments problems.

well as promoting sound economic policies among all its member countries, the IMF is helping to make globalization work for the benefit of all.

The IMF acted swiftly to help countries hit during the Asian financial crisis in 1997–98.

As the development of the world economy since 1945 has brought new challenges, the work of the IMF has evolved and the institution has adapted so as to be able to continue serving its purposes effectively. Especially since the early 1990s, enormous economic challenges have been associated with globalization—the increasing international integration of markets and economies. These have included the need to deal with turbulence in emerging financial markets, notably in Asia and Latin America; to help a number of countries make the transition from central planning to market-oriented systems and enter the global market economy; and to promote economic growth and poverty reduction in the poorest countries at risk of being left behind by globalization.

The IMF has responded partly by introducing reforms aimed at strengthening the architecture—or framework of rules and institutions—of the international monetary and financial system and by enhancing its own contribution to the prevention and resolution of financial crises. It has also given new emphasis to the goals of enhancing economic growth and reducing poverty in the world's poorest countries. And reform is continuing.

In September 2000, at the annual meetings of the IMF and World Bank, the IMF's then Managing Director Horst Köhler set out some major priorities for the work of the IMF, according to which the institution would: strive to promote sustained non-

Adapting to Meet New Challenges

inflationary economic growth that benefits all people of the world; be the center of competence for the stability of the international financial system; focus on its core macroeconomic and financial areas of responsibility, working in a complementary fashion with other institutions established to safeguard global public goods; and be an open institution, learning from experience and dialogue, and adapting continuously to changing circumstances.

These priorities, endorsed by the membership, have been guiding the work and reform of the institution in recent years.

Horst Köhler resigned from the IMF in March 2004 following his nomination for the Presidency of Germany. In May 2004, Rodrigo de Rato, formerly Spain's Vice President for Economic Affairs and Minister of Economy, was selected by the IMF's Executive Board as new Managing Director.

"I see the IMF's main job as promoting financial stability and thereby improving the prospects for sustained growth. By doing so, the IMF also helps the international community in the global war on poverty."

*Rodrigo de Rato,
IMF Managing Director*

The IMF was conceived in July 1944 at an international conference held at Bretton Woods, New Hampshire, U.S.A., when delegates from 44 governments agreed on a framework for economic cooperation partly designed to avoid a repetition of the disastrous economic policies that had contributed to the Great Depression of the 1930s.

During that decade, as economic activity in the major industrial countries weakened, countries attempted to defend their economies by increasing restrictions on imports; but this just worsened the downward spiral in world trade, output, and employment. To conserve dwindling reserves of gold and foreign exchange, some countries curtailed their citizens' freedom to buy abroad, some devalued their currencies, and some introduced complicated restrictions on their citizens' freedom to hold foreign exchange. These fixes, however, also proved self-defeating, and no country was able to maintain its competitive edge for long. Such "beggar-thy-neighbor" policies devastated the international economy; world trade declined sharply, as did employment and living standards in many countries.

As World War II came to a close, the leading allied countries considered various plans to restore order to international

July 1944
The World Bank and the IMF were both conceived at an international conference in Bretton Woods

The Origins of the IMF

monetary relations, and at the Bretton Woods conference the IMF emerged. The country representatives drew up the charter (or Articles of Agreement) of an international institution to oversee the international monetary system and to promote both the elimination of exchange restrictions relating to trade in goods and services, and the stability of exchange rates.

The IMF came into existence in December 1945, when the first 29 countries signed its Articles of Agreement.

The statutory purposes of the IMF today are the same as when they were formulated in 1944 (see Box 2). Since then, the world has experienced unprecedented growth in real incomes. And although the benefits of growth have not flowed equally to all—either within or among nations—most countries have seen increases in prosperity that contrast starkly with the interwar

Architects of the postwar international economic system: U.S. Treasury economist Harry Dexter White (left) meets with British economist John Maynard Keynes

U.S. Treasury Secretary Henry Morgenthau, Jr., addresses the opening of the Bretton Woods Conference

period, in particular. Part of the explanation lies in improvements in the conduct of economic policy, including policies that have encouraged the growth of international trade and helped smooth the economic cycle of boom and bust. The IMF is proud to have contributed to these developments.

Rapid advances in technology and communications have contributed to the increasing global integration of markets

In the decades since World War II, apart from rising prosperity, the world economy and monetary system have undergone other major changes—changes that have increased the importance and relevance of the purposes served by the IMF, but that have also required the IMF to adapt and reform. Rapid advances in technology and communications have contributed to the increasing international integration of markets and to closer linkages among national economies. As a result, financial crises, when they erupt, now tend to spread more rapidly among countries.

In such an increasingly integrated and interdependent world, any country's prosperity depends more than ever both on the economic performance of other countries and on the existence of an open and stable global economic environment. Equally, economic and financial policies that individual countries follow affect how well or how poorly the world trade and payments system operates. Globalization thus calls for greater international cooperation, which in turn has increased the responsibilities of international institutions that organize such cooperation—including the IMF.

The IMF's purposes have also become more important simply because of the expansion of its membership. The number of IMF member countries has more than quadrupled from the 44 states involved in its establishment, reflecting in particular the attainment of political independence by many developing countries and more recently the collapse of the Soviet bloc.

The expansion of the IMF's membership, together with the changes in the world economy, have required the IMF to adapt in a variety of ways to continue serving its purposes effectively.

Box 2
The IMF's Purposes

The purposes of the International Monetary Fund are:

i. To promote international monetary cooperation through a permanent institution which provides the machinery for consultation and collaboration on international monetary problems.

ii. To facilitate the expansion and balanced growth of international trade, and to contribute thereby to the promotion and maintenance of high levels of employment and real income and to the development of the productive resources of all members as primary objectives of economic policy.

iii. To promote exchange stability, to maintain orderly exchange arrangements among members, and to avoid competitive exchange depreciation.

iv. To assist in the establishment of a multilateral system of payments in respect of current transactions between members and in the elimination of foreign exchange restrictions which hamper the growth of world trade.

v. To give confidence to members by making the general resources of the Fund temporarily available to them under adequate safeguards, thus providing them with opportunity to correct maladjustments in their balance of payments without resorting to measures destructive of national or international prosperity.

vi. In accordance with the above, to shorten the duration and lessen the degree of disequilibrium in the international balances of payments of members.

The Fund shall be guided in all its policies and decisions by the purposes set forth in this Article.

From Article I of the IMF's *Articles of Agreement*

Countries that joined the IMF between 1945 and 1971 agreed to keep their exchange rates (in effect, the value of their currencies in terms of the U.S. dollar, and in the case of the United States, the value of the U.S. dollar in terms of gold) pegged at rates that could be adjusted, but only to correct a "fundamental disequilibrium" in the balance of payments and with the IMF's concurrence. This so-called Bretton Woods system of exchange rates prevailed until 1971 when the U.S.

government suspended the convertibility of the U.S. dollar (and dollar reserves held by other governments) into gold. Since then, IMF members have been free to choose any form of exchange arrangement they wish (except pegging their currency to gold): some now allow their currency to float freely, some peg their currency to another currency or a group of currencies, some have adopted the currency of another country as their own, and some participate in currency blocs.

The work of the IMF and the World Bank is complementary

At the same time as the IMF was created, the International Bank for Reconstruction and Development (IBRD), more commonly known as the World Bank, was set up to promote long-term economic development, including through the financing of infrastructure projects, such as road-building and improving water supply.

The IMF and the World Bank Group—which includes the International Finance Corporation (IFC) and the International Development Association (IDA)—complement each other's work. While the IMF's focus is chiefly on macroeconomic performance, and on macroeconomic and financial sector policies, the World Bank is concerned mainly with longer-term development and poverty reduction issues. Its activities include lending to developing countries and countries in transition to finance infrastructure projects, the reform of particular sectors of the economy, and broader structural reforms. The IMF, in contrast, provides financing not for particular sectors or projects but for general support of a country's balance of payments and international reserves while the country takes policy action to address its difficulties.

When the IMF and World Bank were established, an organization to promote world trade liberalization was also contemplated, but it was not until 1995 that the World Trade Organization was set up. In the intervening years, trade issues were tackled through the General Agreement on Tariffs and Trade (GATT).

Who Makes Decisions at the IMF?

The IMF is accountable to its member countries, and this accountability is essential to its effectiveness. The day-to-day work of the IMF is carried out by an Executive Board, representing the IMF's 184 members, and an internationally recruited staff under the leadership of a Managing Director and three Deputy Managing Directors—each member of this management team being drawn from a different region of the world. The powers of the Executive Board to conduct the business of the IMF are delegated to it by the Board of Governors, which is where ultimate oversight rests.

The **Board of Governors**, on which all member countries are represented, is the highest authority governing the IMF. It usually meets once a year, at the Annual Meetings of the IMF and the World Bank. Each member country appoints a Governor—usually the country's minister of finance or the governor of its central bank—and an Alternate Governor. The Board of Governors decides on major policy issues but has delegated day-to-day decision-making to the Executive Board.

Key policy issues relating to the international monetary system are considered twice-yearly in a committee of Governors called the **International Monetary and Financial**

A joint session of the IMFC and the Development Committee meets to discuss global economic trends

Committee, or IMFC (until September 1999 known as the Interim Committee). A joint committee of the Boards of Governors of the IMF and World Bank called the **Development Committee** advises and reports to the Governors on development policy and other matters of concern to developing countries.

The Executive Board consists of 24 Executive Directors, with the Managing Director as chairman. The Executive Board usually meets three times a week, in full-day sessions, and more often if needed, at the organization's headquarters in Washington, D.C. The IMF's five largest shareholders—the United States, Japan, Germany, France, and the United Kingdom—along with China, Russia, and Saudi Arabia, have their own seats on the Board. The other 16 Executive Directors are elected for two-year terms by groups of countries, known as constituencies.

The documents that provide the basis for the Board's deliberations are prepared mainly by IMF staff, sometimes in collaboration with the World Bank, and presented to the Board with management approval; but some documents are presented by Executive Directors themselves. In recent years, an increasing proportion of IMF Board documents have been released to the public through the IMF's website (*www.imf.org*).

Unlike some international organizations that operate under a one-country-one-vote principle (such as the United Nations General Assembly), the IMF has a weighted voting system: the larger a country's quota in the IMF—determined broadly by its economic size— the more votes it has (see "Where Does the IMF Get its Money?" below). But the Board rarely makes decisions based on formal voting; rather, most decisions are based on consensus among its members and are supported unanimously.

The Executive Board selects the **Managing Director**, who besides serving as the chairman of the Board, is the chief of the IMF staff and conducts the business of the IMF under the direction of the Executive Board. Appointed for a renewable five-year term, the Managing Director is assisted by a First Deputy Managing Director and two other Deputy Managing Directors.

IMF employees are international civil servants whose responsibility is to the IMF, not to national authorities. The organization has about 2,800 employees recruited from 141 countries. About two-thirds of its professional staff are economists. The IMF's 26 departments and offices are headed by directors, who report to the Managing Director. Most staff work in Washington, although about 90 resident representatives are posted in member countries to help advise on economic policy. The IMF maintains offices in Paris and Tokyo for liaison with other international and regional institutions, and with organizations of civil society; it also has offices in New York and Geneva, mainly for liaison with other institutions in the UN system.

The IMF employs staff from 141 countries, with most located at its Washington, D.C. headquarters.

The IMF's resources come mainly from the quota (or capital) subscriptions that countries pay when they join the IMF, or following periodic reviews in which quotas are increased. Countries pay 25 percent of their quota subscriptions in Special Drawing Rights (SDRs, see Box 3) or major currencies, such as U.S. dollars or Japanese yen; the IMF can call on the remainder, payable in the member's own currency, to be made available for lending as needed. Quotas determine not only a country's subscription payments, but also the amount of financing that it can receive from the IMF, and its share in SDR allocations. Quotas also are the main determinant of countries' voting power in the IMF.

Quotas determine a country's voting power

Quotas are intended broadly to reflect members' relative size in the world economy: the larger a country's economy in terms of output, and the larger and more variable its trade, the higher its quota tends to be. The United States of America, the world's largest economy, contributes most to the IMF, 17.5 percent of total quotas; Palau, the world's smallest, contributes 0.001 percent. The most recent (eleventh) quota review came

Where Does the IMF Get Its Money?

into effect in January 1999, raising IMF quotas (for the first time since 1990) by about 45 percent to SDR 212 billion (about $300 billion).

If necessary, the IMF may borrow to supplement the resources available from its quotas. The IMF has two sets of standing arrangements to borrow if needed to cope with any threat to the international monetary system:

- the General Arrangements to Borrow (GAB), set up in 1962, which has 11 participants (the governments or central banks of the Group of Ten industrialized countries and Switzerland), and
- the New Arrangements to Borrow (NAB), introduced in 1997, with 25 participating countries and institutions.

Under the two arrangements combined, the IMF has up to SDR 34 billion (about $50 billion) available to borrow.

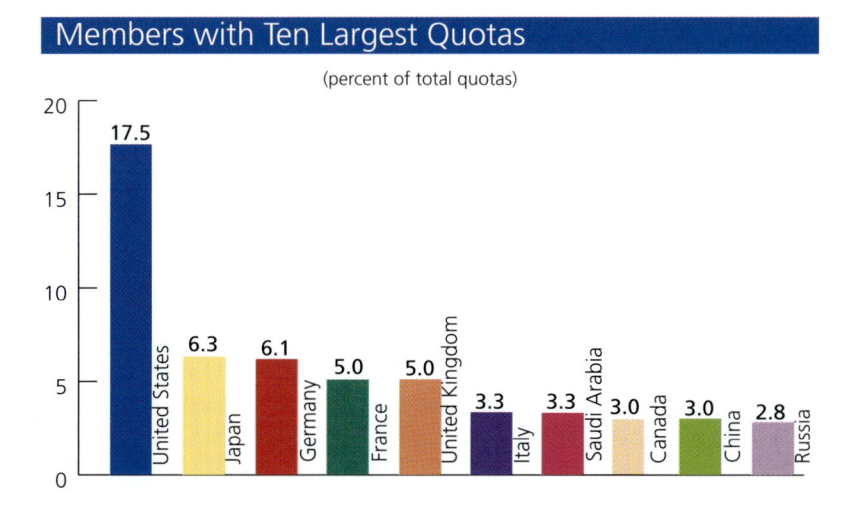

Members with Ten Largest Quotas
(percent of total quotas)

Country	Percent
United States	17.5
Japan	6.3
Germany	6.1
France	5.0
United Kingdom	5.0
Italy	3.3
Saudi Arabia	3.3
Canada	3.0
China	3.0
Russia	2.8

Box 3
What Is an SDR?

The **SDR**, or special drawing right, is an international reserve asset introduced by the IMF in 1969 (under the First Amendment to its Articles of Agreement) out of concern among IMF members that the current stock, and prospective growth, of international reserves might not be sufficient to support the expansion of world trade. The main reserve assets were gold and U.S. dollars, and members did not want global reserves to depend on gold production, with its inherent uncertainties, and continuing U.S. balance of payments deficits, which would be needed to provide continuing growth in U.S. dollar reserves. The SDR was introduced as a supplementary reserve asset, which the IMF could "allocate" periodically to members when the need arose, and cancel, as necessary.

SDRs—sometimes known as "paper gold" although they have no physical form—have been allocated to member countries (as bookkeeping entries) as a percentage of their quotas. So far, the IMF has allocated SDR 21.4 billion (about $32 billion) to member countries. The last allocation took place in 1981, when SDR 4.1 billion was allocated to the 141 countries that were then members of the IMF. Since 1981, the membership has not seen a need for another general allocation of SDRs, partly because of the growth of international capital markets. In September 1997, however, in light of the IMF's expanded membership—which included countries that had not received an allocation—the Board of Governors proposed a Fourth Amendment to the Articles of Agreement. When approved by the required majority of member governments, this will authorize a special one-time "equity" allocation of SDR 21.4 billion, to be distributed so as to raise all members' ratios of cumulative SDR allocations to quotas to a common benchmark.

IMF member countries may use SDRs in transactions among themselves, with 16 "institutional" holders of SDRs, and with the IMF. The SDR is also the IMF's unit of account. A number of other international and regional organizations and international conventions use it as a unit of account, or as a basis for a unit of account.

The SDR's value is set daily using a basket of four major currencies: the euro, Japanese yen, pound sterling, and U.S. dollar. On July 1, 2004, SDR 1 = US$1.48. The composition of the basket is reviewed every five years to ensure that it is representative of the currencies used in international transactions, and that the weights assigned to the currencies reflect their relative importance in the world's trading and financial systems.

How Does the IMF Serve Its Members?

The IMF helps its member countries by:

- reviewing and monitoring national and global economic and financial developments and advising members on their economic policies; 
- lending them hard currencies to support adjustment and reform policies designed to correct balance of payments problems and promote sustainable growth; and 
- offering a wide range of technical assistance, as well as training for government and central bank officials, in its areas of expertise.

Advice on Policies and Global Oversight

The IMF's Articles of Agreement call for it to oversee the international monetary system, including by exercising firm "surveillance"—that is, oversight—over its member countries' exchange rate policies. Under the Articles, each member country undertakes to collaborate with the IMF in its efforts to ensure orderly exchange arrangements and to promote a stable system of exchange rates.

More specifically, member countries agree to direct policies toward the goals of orderly economic growth with reasonable price stability, together with orderly underlying economic and financial conditions, and to avoid manipulating exchange rates for unfair competitive advantage. In addition, each country undertakes to provide the IMF with the information necessary for its effective surveillance. The membership has agreed that the IMF's surveillance of each member's exchange rate policies has to be carried out within the framework of a comprehensive analysis of the general economic situation and economic policy strategy of the member.

The regular monitoring of economies, and associated provision of policy advice, that IMF surveillance involves can help signal dangers ahead and enable members to act in a timely way to avoid trouble.

The IMF conducts its oversight in three ways:

Country surveillance, which takes the form of regular (usually yearly) comprehensive consultations with individual member countries about their economic policies, with interim discussions as needed. The consultations are referred to as *"Article IV consultations"* as they are mandated by Article IV of the IMF's charter. (They are also referred to as "bilateral" consultations, but this is strictly speaking a misnomer: when the IMF consults with a member country, it represents the entire membership, so that the consultations are really always multilateral.)

The IMF can help signal economic dangers ahead and enable members to act to avoid trouble

How does an Article IV consultation proceed? First, an IMF team of economists visits the country to collect economic and financial data and discuss with government and central bank officials the country's economic policies in the context of recent developments. The IMF staff review the country's macroeconomic (fiscal, monetary, and exchange rate) policies, assess the soundness of the financial system, and examine industrial, social, labor, governance, environmental, and other policy issues that may affect macroeconomic policies and performance. The staff team then submits a report on its findings, approved by management, to the Executive Board, which discusses the staff's analysis. And the Board's views, summarized by its Chairman, are transmitted to the country's government. In this way, the views of the global community and the lessons of international experience are brought to bear on the policies of the country concerned.

With the increased transparency of the IMF and its work in recent years, the summings up of Board discussions for many Article IV consultations are being published, together with summaries of the staff's analysis, in Public Information Notices (PINs). In fact, in many cases, the full staff reports prepared for these consultations are also being released. Like PINs, they can be found on the IMF's website.

The IMF supplements its usually annual country consultations with additional staff visits to member countries when needed. The Executive Board also holds frequent, informal meetings to review economic and financial developments in selected member countries and regions.

Global surveillance, which entails reviews by the IMF's Executive Board of global economic trends and developments. The main reviews of this kind are based on *World Economic Outlook* and *Global Financial Stability* reports prepared by IMF staff, normally twice a year, before the semiannual meetings of the International Monetary and Financial Committee. The reports are published in full prior to the IMFC meetings, together with the Chairman's summing up of the Executive Board's discussion. The Executive Board also holds more frequent, informal discussions on world economic and market developments.

Regional surveillance, under which the IMF examines policies pursued under regional arrangements. This includes, for example, Board discussions of developments in the European Union, the euro area, the West African Economic and Monetary Union, the Central African Economic and Monetary Community, and the Eastern Caribbean Currency Union.

IMF management and staff also participate in surveillance discussions of such groups of countries as the G–7 (the Group of Seven major industrial countries) and APEC (the Asia-Pacific Economic Cooperation forum).

Lending to Help Countries in Difficulty

The IMF lends foreign exchange to countries with balance of payments problems. An IMF loan eases the adjustment that a country has to make to bring its spending in line with its income so as to correct its balance of payments problem. But IMF lending is also intended to support policies, including structural reforms, that will improve a country's balance of payments position and growth prospects in a lasting way.

Any member country can turn to the IMF for financing if it has a balance of payments need—that is, if it needs official borrowing to be able to make external payments and maintain an appropriate level of reserves without taking "measures destructive of national or international prosperity." Such measures might include restrictions on trade and payments, a sharp compression of demand in the domestic economy, or a sharp depreciation of the domestic currency. Without IMF lending, countries with balance of payments difficulties would have to adjust more abruptly or take such other measures damaging to national and international prosperity. Avoiding such consequences is among the IMF's purposes (see Box 2, (v) and (vi)).

Any member country with a balance of payments problem can turn to the IMF for financing

What Is an IMF-Supported Program?

When a country approaches the IMF for financing, it may be in a state of economic crisis or near-crisis, with its currency under attack in foreign exchange markets and its international reserves depleted, economic activity stagnant or falling, and bankruptcies increasing. To return the country's external payments position to health and to restore the conditions for sustainable economic growth, some combination of economic adjustment and official and/or private financing will be needed.

The IMF provides the country's authorities with advice on the economic policies that may be expected to address the problems most effectively. For the IMF also to provide financing, it must agree with the authorities on a program of policies aimed at meeting specific, quantified goals regarding external viability, monetary and financial stability, and sustainable growth. Details of the program are spelled out in a **"letter of intent"** from the government to the Managing Director of the IMF.

A program supported by IMF financing is designed by the national authorities in close cooperation with IMF staff, and is tailored to the special needs and circumstances of the country. This is essential for the program's effectiveness and for the government to win national support for the program. Such support—or "local ownership"—of the program is critical to its success.

Each program is also designed flexibly, so that, during its implementation, it may be reassessed and revised if circumstances change. Many programs are, in fact, revised during implementation.

Instruments of IMF lending and their evolution

The IMF provides loans under a variety of policies or "facilities" that have evolved over the years to meet the needs of the membership. The duration, repayment terms, and lending conditions attached to these facilities vary, reflecting the types of balance of payments problem and circumstances they address (see Box 4 on page 27).

Top 12 IMF Borrowers, 1947–2000

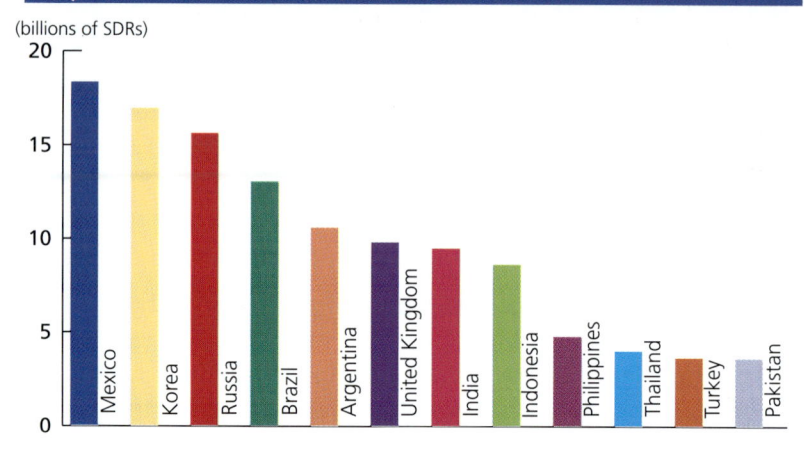

(billions of SDRs)

Mexico, Korea, Russia, Brazil, Argentina, United Kingdom, India, Indonesia, Philippines, Thailand, Turkey, Pakistan

Most of the IMF's financing is provided through three different types of lending policies:

The Stand-By Arrangement helps countries with short-term balance of payments problems

Stand-By Arrangements form the core of the IMF's lending policies. First used in 1952, they are designed to deal mainly with short-term balance of payments problems.

Medium-term extended arrangements under the **Extended Fund Facility** are intended for countries with balance of payments difficulties related to structural problems, which may take longer to correct than macroeconomic weaknesses. Structural policies associated with extended arrangements include reforms designed to improve the way economies function, such as tax and financial sector reforms, privatization of public enterprises, and steps to enhance the flexibility of labor markets.

The IMF has been providing concessional lending to help its poorest member countries achieve external viability, sustainable economic growth, and improved living standards since the late 1970s. The current concessional facility, the **Poverty Reduction and Growth Facility** (PRGF), replaced the Enhanced Structural Adjustment Facility (ESAF) in November 1999, with the aim of making poverty reduction and economic growth the central objectives of policy programs in the countries concerned.

In the late 1990s, the IMF introduced facilities designed to help countries cope with sudden losses of market confidence, and to prevent "contagion"—the spread of financial crises to countries with sound economic policies. (See pages 30–33 for highlights of the IMF's evolving facilities.) The IMF also provides loans to help countries cope with balance of payments problems caused by natural disasters, the aftermath of military conflicts, and temporary shortfalls in export earnings (or temporary increases in cereal import costs) beyond their control.

Just as new facilities have been introduced to meet new challenges, redundant facilities have over time been terminated. Indeed, the Executive Board initiated in early 2000 a review of facilities (for the main IMF lending facilities, see Box 4). The review led to the elimination of four obsolete facilities. The Board's consideration of modifications to other nonconcessional facilities led to agreement to:

- adapt the terms of Stand-By Arrangements and Extended Fund Facility loans to encourage countries to avoid reliance on IMF resources for unduly long periods or in unduly large amounts;
- reaffirm the Extended Fund Facility as one confined to cases where longer-term financing is clearly required; and
- enhance monitoring of IMF-supported programs after their expiration, especially when a member's credit outstanding exceeds a certain threshold.

The IMF has assisted the countries of the former Soviet Union in their transition from centrally planned to market economies

At present, IMF borrowers are all either developing countries, countries in transition from central planning to market-based systems, or emerging market countries recovering from financial crises. Many of these countries have only limited access to international capital markets, partly because of their economic difficulties. Since the late 1970s, all industrial countries have been able to meet their financing needs from capital markets, but in the first two decades of the IMF's existence over half of the IMF's financing went to these countries.

Key features of IMF lending

- The IMF is not an aid agency or a development bank. It lends to help its members tackle balance of payments problems and restore sustainable economic growth. The foreign exchange provided, the limits on which are set in relation to a member's quota in the IMF, is deposited with the country's central bank to supplement its international reserves and thus to give general balance of payments support. Unlike the loans of development agencies, IMF funds are not provided to finance particular projects or activities.

- IMF lending is **conditional** on policies: the borrowing country must adopt policies that promise to correct its balance of payments problem. The conditionality associated with IMF lending helps to ensure that by borrowing from the IMF, a country does not just postpone hard choices and accumulate more debt, but is able to strengthen its economy and repay the loan. The country and the IMF must agree on the economic policy actions that are needed. Also the IMF disburses funds in phases, linked to the borrowing country's meeting its scheduled policy commitments. During 2000–01 the IMF worked to **streamline** its conditionality— making it more sharply focused on macroeconomic and financial

Box 4

Selected IMF Lending Facilities

Stand-By Arrangements form the core of the IMF's lending policies. A Stand-By Arrangement provides assurance to a member country that it can draw up to a specified amount, usually over 12–18 months, to deal with a short-term balance of payments problem.

Extended Fund Facility. IMF support for members under the Extended Fund Facility provides assurance that a member country can draw up to a specified amount, usually over three to four years, to help it tackle structural economic problems that are causing serious weaknesses in its balance of payments.

Poverty Reduction and Growth Facility (which replaced the *Enhanced Structural Adjustment Facility* in November 1999). A low-interest facility to help the poorest member countries facing protracted balance of payments problems (see page 46, "A New Approach to Reducing Poverty"). The cost to borrowers is subsidized with resources raised through past sales of IMF-owned gold, together with loans and grants provided to the IMF for the purpose by its members.

Supplemental Reserve Facility. Provides additional short-term financing to member countries experiencing exceptional balance of payments difficulty because of a sudden and disruptive loss of market confidence reflected in capital outflows. The interest rate on SRF loans includes a surcharge over the IMF's usual lending rate.

Emergency Assistance. Introduced in 1962 to help members cope with balance of payments problems arising from sudden and unforeseeable natural disasters, this form of assistance was extended in 1995 to cover certain situations in which members have emerged from military conflicts that have disrupted institutional and administrative capacity.

sector policies, less intrusive into countries' policy choices, more conducive to country ownership of policy programs, and thus more effective.

- IMF lending is **temporary**. Depending on the lending facility used, loans may be disbursed over periods as short as six months and as long as four years. The repayment period is 3¼–5 years for short-term loans (under Stand-By Arrangements), or 4½–10 years for medium-term financing (under Extended Arrangements); but in November 2000, the

Executive Board agreed to introduce the expectation of earlier repayment—over 2¼–4 years for Stand-By Arrangements and 4½–7 years for Extended Arrangements. The repayment period for loans to low-income countries under the IMF's concessional lending facility, the PRGF, is 10 years, with a 5½-year grace period on principal payments.

• The IMF expects borrowers to give priority to repaying its loans. The borrowing country must **pay back** the IMF on schedule, so that the funds are available for lending to other countries that need balance of payments financing. The IMF has in place procedures to deter the build-up of any arrears, or overdue repayments and interest charges. Most important, however, is the weight that the international community places on the IMF's status as a preferred creditor. This ensures that the IMF is among the first to be repaid even though it is often the last lender willing to provide a country with funds, after the country's ability to fulfil its obligation has clearly come into question.

- Countries that borrow from the IMF's regular, non-concessional lending windows—all but the low-income developing countries—pay **market-related** interest rates and service charges, plus a refundable commitment fee. A surcharge can be levied above a certain threshold to discourage heavy use of IMF funds. Surcharges also apply to drawings under the Supplemental Reserve Facility. Low-income countries borrowing under the Poverty Reduction and Growth Facility pay a **concessional** fixed interest rate of ½ percent a year.

- To strengthen **safeguards** on members' use of IMF resources, in March 2000 the IMF began requiring assessments of central banks' compliance with desirable practices for internal control procedures, financial reporting, and audit mechanisms. At the same time, the Executive Board decided to broaden the application, and make more systematic use, of the available tools to deal with countries that borrow from the IMF on the basis of erroneous information.

- In most cases, the IMF, when it lends, provides only a small portion of a country's external financing requirements. But because the approval of IMF lending signals that a country's economic policies are on the right track, it reassures investors and the official community and helps generate additional financing from these sources. Thus, IMF financing can act as an important lever, or catalyst, for attracting other funds. The IMF's ability to perform this **catalytic role** is based on the confidence that other lenders have in its operations and especially in the credibility of the policy conditionality attached to its lending.

> By endorsing a country's policies, the IMF reassures investors and helps generate additional financing

29

Highlights in the Evol

1952

Stand-By Arrangements were introduced in 1952. Belgium was the first user when it sought $50 million from the IMF to bolster its international reserves. The term "stand-by" means that, subject to conditionality, a member has a right to draw the money made available if needed. In most cases, the member does in fact draw.

1963

In 1963, the IMF set up a **Compensatory Financing Facility** to help member countries that produce primary commodities cope with temporary shortfalls in export earnings, including as a result of price declines. An additional component to help countries deal with temporary rises in cereal import costs was added in 1981.

1970s

At the time of the energy crisis in the 1970s, when oil prices quadrupled, the IMF helped recycle the foreign currency surpluses of oil-exporting countries through a temporary **Oil Facility**, in effect from 1974 to 1976. It borrowed from oil exporters and other countries in a strong external position and lent to oil importers to help finance their oil-related deficits.

ution of IMF Lending

1974

In 1974, the **Extended Fund Facility** was established to provide medium-term assistance to members suffering balance of payments problems related to structural weaknesses in their economies, requiring structural reforms over an extended period. The length of extended arrangements is typically three years, with possible extension for a fourth year. The first EFF arrangement was with Kenya in 1975.

1980s

In the 1980s, the IMF played a central role in helping resolve the Latin American **debt crisis,** working with national governments and the international banking community. The IMF helped debtor countries design medium-term stabilization programs, provided substantial financing from its own resources, and arranged financing packages from creditor governments, commercial banks, and international organizations.

1989

Since 1989, the IMF has actively helped countries in central and eastern Europe, the Baltics, Russia, and other countries of the former Soviet Union transform their economies **from centrally planned to market-oriented systems.** It has worked in partnership with these countries to help stabilize and restructure their economies—including, for example, helping them build the legal and institutional framework of a market system. To provide additional financing to support the early stages of transition, the IMF established a *Systemic Transformation Facility* in 1993, which lapsed in 1995.

Lending Highlights

1994–95

In 1994–95, **Mexico** faced a severe financial crisis when a shift in market sentiment led to sudden, large capital outflows. Mexico quickly adopted a strong and ultimately successful program of adjustment and reform. In support of the program, the IMF swiftly approved its largest loan to date of $17.8 billion. It also led the IMF to set up the New Arrangements to Borrow (NAB) to ensure the IMF would have sufficient funds to respond to major crises in the future.

1996

In 1996, the IMF and the World Bank jointly launched the *Initiative for the Heavily Indebted Poor Countries*, known as the **HIPC Initiative**, with the aim of reducing the external debt of the world's poorest to sustainable levels in a reasonably short period. The Initiative was enhanced in 1999 to provide faster, broader, and deeper debt relief. At the same time, the IMF replaced its concessional *Enhanced Structural Adjustment Facility* (introduced in 1987) with the *Poverty Reduction and Growth Facility*, which gave more explicit attention to poverty reduction (see page 46, "A New Approach to Reducing Poverty in Low-Income Countries").

1997–98

During the **Asian financial crisis** of 1997–98, the IMF provided exceptionally large loans—totaling more than $36 billion—to Indonesia, Korea, and Thailand in support of stabilization policies and structural reforms. The IMF created the *Supplemental Reserve Facility* in 1997 specifically to help countries deal with large short-term financing needs stemming from a sudden loss of market confidence reflected in capital outflows.

2000

In November 2000, the IMF's Executive Board concluded **a major review of IMF financial facilities** to assess whether the ways in which IMF financial assistance is provided to members needed modification. This effort produced a significant streamlining through the elimination of four facilities. A number of other important changes were implemented that should allow IMF facilities to play a more effective role in supporting members' efforts to prevent and resolve crises and to help ensure a more efficient use of IMF resources.

2004

IMF sets up **Trade Integration Mechanism** to help cushion the short-term adverse impact of trade liberalization on small developing countries as they embrace a more competitive international environment.

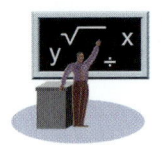

Technical Assistance and Training

The IMF is probably best known for its policy advice and its policy-based lending to countries in times of economic crisis. But the IMF also shares its expertise with member countries on a regular basis by providing technical assistance and training in a wide range of areas, such as central banking, monetary and exchange rate policy, tax policy and administration, and official statistics. The objective is to help strengthen the design and implementation of members' economic policies, including by strengthening skills in the institutions responsible, such as finance ministries and central banks. Technical assistance complements the IMF's policy advice and financial assistance to member countries and accounts for some 20 percent of the IMF's administrative costs.

Technical assistance complements the IMF's policy advice and financial assistance

The IMF began providing technical assistance in the mid-1960s when many newly independent countries sought help in setting up their central banks and finance ministries. Another surge in technical assistance occurred in the early 1990s, when countries in central and eastern Europe and the former Soviet Union began their shift from centrally planned to market-based economic systems. More recently, the IMF has stepped up its provision of technical assistance as part of the effort to strengthen the architecture of the international financial system.

Specifically, it has been helping countries bolster their financial systems, improve the collection and dissemination of economic and financial data, strengthen their tax and legal systems, and improve banking regulation and supervision. It has also given considerable operational advice to countries that have had to reestablish government institutions following severe civil unrest or war.

The IMF provides technical assistance and training mainly in four areas:

- strengthening monetary and financial sectors through advice on banking system regulation, supervision, and restructuring, foreign exchange management and operations, clearing and settlement systems for payments, and the structure and development of central banks;

- supporting strong fiscal policies and management through advice on tax and customs policies and administration, budget formulation, expenditure management, design of social safety nets, and the management of internal and external debt;

- compiling, managing, and disseminating statistical data and improving data quality; and

- drafting and reviewing economic and financial legislation.

The IMF offers training courses for government and central bank officials of member countries at its headquarters in Washington and at regional training centers in Brasília, Singapore, Tunis, and Vienna. In the field, it provides technical assistance through visits by IMF staff, supplemented by hired consultants and experts. Supplementary financing for IMF technical assistance and training is provided by the national governments of such countries as Japan and Switzerland, and international agencies such as the European Union, the Organization for Economic Cooperation and Development, the United Nations Development Program, and the World Bank.

IMF Technical Assistance By Region
(Fiscal year 2001)

- Latin America Caribbean (10%)
- Middle East (11%)
- Asia (23%)
- Africa (27%)
- Europe (29%)

Strengthening the International

Globalization has created new challenges for the IMF. Two of the most important, and most difficult, are how to strengthen the global financial system—so that it becomes less prone to financial crises and more able to cope with crises when they occur—and how to advance the fight against poverty in low-income countries (see next chapter).

Globalization has yielded great benefits for many countries and people around the world. Integration into the world economy is an essential part of any strategy to enable countries to

Monetary and Financial System

achieve higher living standards. But globalization, by increasing the volume and speed of international capital flows, has also increased the risk of financial crises. And at the same time, the risk has arisen that low-income countries, which have not yet benefited substantially from globalization, will fall further behind as living standards rise elsewhere.

Building A Stronger Global Financial System

The financial crises in emerging markets in the mid- and late 1990s were a reminder of the risks associated with globalization—even for economies that have benefited immensely from the process and that, in many respects, are well managed. The economies hit in the 1997–98 Asian crisis, in particular, had gained enormously over several decades from international trade, foreign direct investment, and access to increasingly integrated international financial markets. The crises exposed not only policy weaknesses in the crisis countries themselves, but also flaws in the international financial system, driving home two facts of life:

- Investors may retreat quickly and massively if they sense shortcomings in domestic economic policies. Once investors—domestic or foreign—lose confidence, capital inflows can dry up, and large net outflows can precipitate a financial crisis.

- A crisis in one country or region can rapidly spill over into other economies.

To reduce the risk of future financial crises and to promote the speedy resolution of those that do occur, the IMF has been working with its member governments, and with other international organizations, regulatory bodies, and the private sector, to strengthen the international monetary and financial system.

Reforms under way span the following areas:

Strengthening financial sectors

A major reason why a country may be vulnerable to economic crisis is weakness in its financial system, with institutions that are illiquid or insolvent, or liable to become so as a result of adverse developments. To make the system more robust, banks and other financial institutions may need to improve their internal controls, including their assessment and management of risk. The authorities may also need to bring their supervision and regulation of the financial sector up to international standards.

Integration into the world economy is an essential part of any strategy to raise living standards

The IMF and the World Bank in 1999 began joint assessments of member countries' financial sectors to help identify actual and potential weaknesses. IMF and World Bank teams, generally with the assistance of experts from central banks and financial regulatory agencies, have been assessing the strength of financial systems in a number of member countries. These assessments are presented to the country as a guide to the measures needed.

IMF staff are also working with national governments and other international institutions to:

- strengthen the legal, regulatory, and supervisory frameworks for banks,
- review minimum capital requirements for banks and financial institutions,
- develop a core set of international accounting standards,
- finalize a set of core principles for good corporate governance,

- avoid exchange rate regimes that are vulnerable to attack, and
- ensure a freer flow of timely financial data to markets.

Similarly, the IMF has been working with the Basel Committee on Banking Supervision to improve regulatory standards.

Internationally accepted standards and codes of good practice

Countries can reassure the international community about their policies and practices by following internationally accepted standards and codes of good practice. For countries that do not do so, international standards and codes serve as a guide for strengthening their systems. The IMF has worked to develop and refine voluntary standards in areas of its responsibility, in some cases cooperating with other international organizations, such as the Bank for International Settlements (BIS) and the World Bank. These include standards related to a country's statistical practices; codes of good practice in fiscal,

The IMF is working with member governments to help them meet international standards and codes of good practice

monetary, and financial policies; and guidelines on strengthening the financial sector—such as banking system supervision and regulatory standards.

Complementing the work of the IMF have been the efforts of the BIS, World Bank, and other standard-setting agencies, which have been working on international standards in such areas as accounting and auditing, bankruptcy, corporate governance, securities market regulation, and payment and settlement systems.

To help countries assess their own compliance, IMF staff, in conjunction with the respective governments, began in 1999 to prepare experimental country reports on countries' observance of standards and codes, focusing mainly on areas of direct operational concern to the IMF. Several countries have chosen to publish these reports.

Encouraging openness and publication of data

The publication of up-to-date and reliable data—as well as information about countries' economic and financial policies, practices, and decision-making—is needed to help investors make informed judgments and for markets to operate efficiently and smoothly. In the wake of the Mexican crisis of 1994–95, the IMF in 1996 devel-

Markets need up-to-date and reliable data to operate efficiently

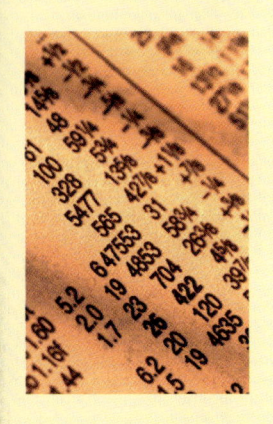

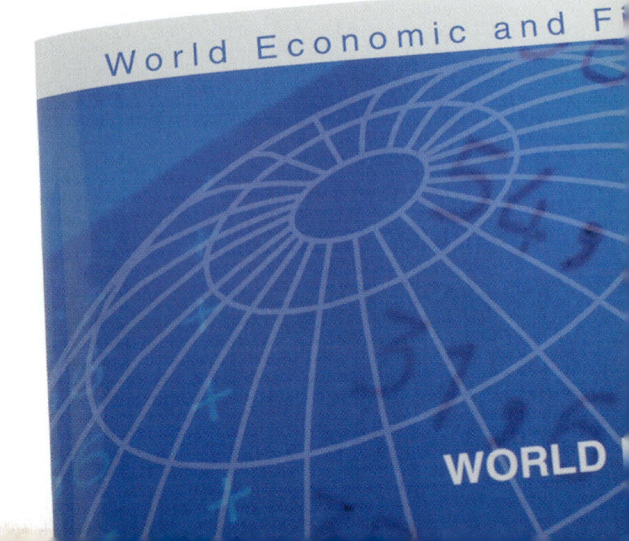

oped a special data dissemination standard (SDDS) to guide countries that have, or that might seek, access to international capital markets in the dissemination of economic and financial data to the public. Subscribing countries agree to publish detailed national economic and financial data, including data on international reserves and external debt, on an announced schedule. A general data dissemination system (GDDS) was established in 1997 to guide countries that are not yet in a position to subscribe to the SDDS and need to improve their statistical systems.

IMF transparency and accountability

Improved provision of information to the markets and the broader public is a central element of the reform of the international financial system. It is also a cornerstone of the recent and continuing reform of the IMF itself.

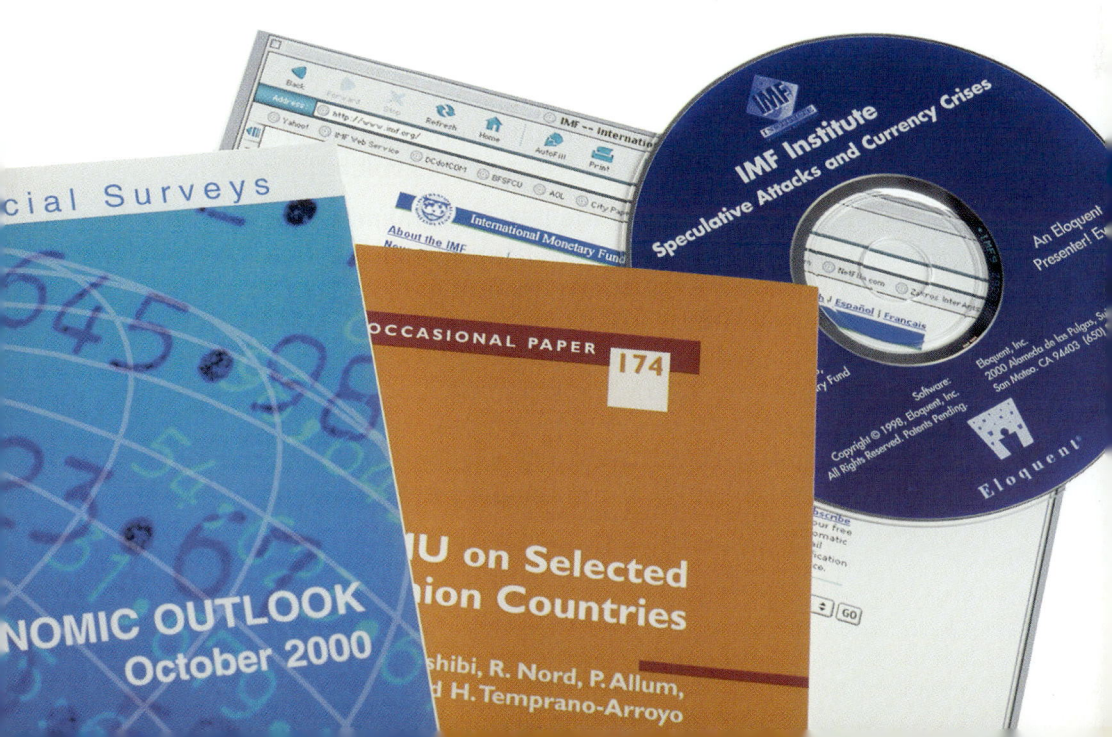

Transparency, on the part of IMF member countries and the IMF, helps foster better economic performance in several ways. Greater openness by member countries encourages more widespread and better informed analysis of their policies by the public; enhances the accountability of policymakers and the credibility of policies; and informs financial markets so that they can function in a more orderly and efficient manner. Greater openness and clarity by the IMF about its own policies, and the advice it gives members, contribute to a more informed policy debate and to a better understanding of the IMF's role and operations. By exposing its advice to public scrutiny and debate, the IMF can also help raise the level of its analysis.

Since the mid-1990s, the IMF has vastly increased the volume of information it publishes—on its own activities and policies, and on those of its member countries—particularly on its website. Public Information Notices, for example, which were released at the conclusion of Article IV consultations with about 80 percent of member countries in 1999–2000, summarize the Executive Board discussion and provide background to the consultation. Letters of intent are also released by the governments concerned in about 80 percent of program cases. In April 1999, the Executive Board initiated a pilot project for the voluntary release of Article IV staff reports, and about 60 countries agreed to such release over the following 18 months. In November 2000, the pilot was replaced by a publication policy providing for voluntary release (that is, subject to the agreement of the country concerned) of both Article IV consultation papers and papers on members' use of IMF resources. In July 2004, the policy was revised to introduce the presumption that these papers would be released on a voluntary basis.

The IMF has vastly increased the amount of information it publishes

The accountability of the IMF, to its member governments and to the broader public, has been enhanced in recent years through external evaluations by outside experts of its policies and activities. Published external evaluations include assessments of the Enhanced Structural Adjustment Facility (which was replaced in 1999 by the Poverty Reduction and Growth Facility), its surveillance of members' economies, and IMF economic research activities. An Independent Evaluation Office was established in 2001, and released three evaluation reports during 2002–03.

While increasing the transparency of the IMF, the Executive Board is also keenly aware of the need to preserve the IMF's role as a confidential advisor to its members, which continues to be an essential part of its role.

Involving the private sector in crisis prevention and resolution

By far the greater part of international financial flows are private flows. This points to the importance of the role that the private sector can play in helping to prevent and resolve financial crises. Crises may be prevented, and the volatility of private flows reduced, by improved risk assessment and closer and more frequent dialogue between countries and private investors. Such dialogue can also foster greater private sector involvement in the resolution of crises when they do occur, including through the restructuring of private debt.

Both creditors and debtors can benefit from such dialogue. And the involvement of the private sector in crisis prevention and resolution should also help to limit "moral hazard"—that is, the possibility that the private sector may be attracted to engage in risky lending if it is confident that potential losses will be limited by official rescue operations, including by the IMF.

The IMF tracks developments in capital markets through its International Capital Markets Department, set up in 2001

Improved risk assessment and improved dialogue between debtors and creditors can help prevent crises

The IMF itself is also strengthening its dialogue with market participants, for example through the establishment of the Capital Markets Consultative Group, which met for the first time in September 2000. The Group provides a forum for regular communication between international capital market participants and IMF management and senior staff on matters of common interest, including world economic and market developments and measures to strengthen the global financial system. But the Group does not discuss confidential matters related to particular countries.

When crises do occur, IMF-supported programs are expected to be able, in most cases, to restore stability through their mix of official financing, policy adjustments, and associated gains in confidence among private investors. In certain cases, however, such actions as coordinated debt restructuring by private creditors may be needed. IMF members have agreed on some principles to guide the involvement of the private sector in crisis resolution. These principles, however, require further development, and they will need to be applied flexibly in individual country cases.

Collaborating with other institutions

The IMF collaborates actively with the World Bank, the regional development banks, the World Trade Organization, the United Nations agencies, and other international bodies. Each of these institutions has its area of specialization and its particular contribution to make to the world economy. The IMF's collaboration with the World Bank on poverty reduction is especially close because the Bank rather than the IMF has the expertise to help countries improve their social policies (see next section).

Other areas in which the IMF and World Bank are working closely include assessments of member countries' financial sectors aimed at pinpointing systemic vulnerabilities, combating money laundering and the financing of terrorism, the development of standards and codes, and improving the quality, availability, and coverage of data on external debt.

The IMF and World Bank work together to assess members' financial sectors

The IMF is also a member of the Financial Stability Forum, which brings together national authorities responsible for financial stability in significant international financial centers, international regulatory and supervisory bodies, committees of central bank experts, and international financial institutions.

Refugees line up at a UN post in Timor-Leste (former East Timor). The IMF has worked closely with the UN to revive economic activity in Timor-Leste and help set up financial institutions

A New Approach to Reducing

The IMF is a monetary, not a development, institution, but it has an important role to play in reducing poverty in its member countries: sustainable economic growth, which is essential for cutting poverty, requires sound macroeconomic policies, and these are at the heart of the IMF's mandate.

For many years, the IMF has helped low-income countries implement economic policies that foster growth and raise living standards through its advice, its technical assistance, and its financial support. Between 1986 and 1999, 56 countries with populations totalling 3.2 billion drew on low-interest loans under the Structural Adjustment Facility (SAF) (1986–87) and its successor, the Enhanced Structural Adjustment Facility (ESAF) (1987–89) (see page 27), designed to help the IMF's poorest members in their efforts to achieve stronger economic growth and a sustained improvement in their balance of payments.

Poverty in Low-Income Countries

These facilities made significant contributions to the development effort in low-income countries, but despite substantial assistance from the IMF and the broad donor community, many of these countries did not achieve the gains needed for lasting poverty reduction.

This prompted an intense reexamination of development and debt strategies in recent years by governments, international organizations, and others. It was agreed that more needed to be done.

At the 1999 joint annual meeting of the IMF and the World Bank, Ministers from member countries endorsed a new approach. They decided to make country-generated poverty reduction strategies the basis of all IMF and World Bank concessional lending and debt relief. This embodied a more country-driven approach to policy programs than in the past.

Poverty reduction strategies can put countries "in the driver's seat" of their own development

The New Approach: a focus on serving the poor

Focused poverty reduction strategies can ensure that the needs of the poor get first priority in the public policy debate, especially when there is broad participation—including elements of civil society—in formulating the strategy. Moreover, poverty reduction strategies can put countries "in the driver's seat" of their own development, with a clearly articulated vision for their future and a systematic plan to achieve their goals. Underlying the new approach are a number of principles, which have guided the development of poverty reduction strategies.

These include:

- A comprehensive approach to development and a broad view of poverty are essential.
- Faster economic growth is critical for sustained poverty reduction, and greater participation by the poor can increase a country's growth potential.
- Country "ownership" of the goals, strategy, and direction of development and poverty reduction is vital.
- The development community must work together closely.
- The focus should be clearly on results.

A transformation of the magnitude being sought entails changing institutions so that they are accountable to all, including the poor, and building each country's capacity to respond to the needs of its citizens. Results will come only if there is a long-term commitment by governments and their partners. To help achieve this, participating countries draw up a master plan embodied in a **Poverty Reduction Strategy Paper** (PRSP). This overall plan for reducing poverty makes it easier for the international community—including the IMF—to provide the most effective support possible.

The Roles of the IMF and World Bank

The World Bank and IMF make support available to governments in the development of their strategies, but without directing the outcome. World Bank and IMF management realize that this requires a shift in the organizational cultures and attitude both in these organizations and in partner institutions. This shift is taking place. By coordinating early and maintaining open lines of communication with country authorities—particularly by providing available diagnostic information—the World Bank and IMF can ensure that they help countries in a timely and comprehensive way.

Each institution must focus on its areas of expertise. Thus, World Bank staff take the lead in advising on the social policies involved in poverty reduction, including the necessary diagnostic work. The IMF advises governments in the areas of its traditional mandate, including promoting prudent macroeconomic policies. In areas where the World Bank and the IMF both have expertise—such as fiscal management, budget execution, budget transparency, and tax and customs administration—they coordinate closely.

Because the PRSP provides the context for IMF and World Bank concessional lending and debt relief, the strategies are critical for the two institutions. Participating countries send the final strategy to the Executive Boards of both the IMF and World Bank for endorsement. The Executive Boards of both institutions also receive a World Bank-IMF staff assessment, with an analysis of the strategy and a recommendation on endorsement. The strategies need not be fully in accordance with staff recommendations to be endorsed. This process assures the Executive Boards—and the international community—that the strategies, while perhaps attracting broad domestic support, also address difficult or divisive issues in an effective way.

The Poverty Reduction Strategy Paper promotes coherence in policies

A crowded classroom in Tanzania. Without stronger growth, many countries in Africa are unlikely to achieve the U.N.'s Millennium Development Goals, including for education.

Box 5
Formulating Poverty Reduction Strategies

The objective of drawing up a Poverty Reduction Strategy Paper (PRSP) is to strengthen basic principles of country ownership, comprehensive development, and broad public participation. While there is no template for this, there are a number of core elements that are likely to be common to all strategies.

Diagnosing obstacles to poverty reduction and growth. A poverty reduction strategy could begin by using existing data to describe who the poor are and where they live, and by identifying areas where data need to be strengthened. Building on this description, the poverty reduction strategy could analyze the macroeconomic, social, and institutional impediments to faster growth and poverty reduction.

Policies and objectives. In light of a deeper understanding of poverty and its causes, the PRSP can then identify medium- and long-term targets for the country's poverty reduction strategy and set out the macroeconomic, structural, and social policies to achieve them.

Tracking progress. To understand better the link between policies and outcomes, a poverty reduction strategy should include a framework for monitoring progress and mechanisms to share this information with a country's development partners.

External assistance. A strategy can also improve the effectiveness and efficiency of external assistance by identifying the amount of financial and technical support required to implement the strategy. It could also assess the potential poverty impact of both higher and lower assistance commitments, including actual savings from debt relief.

Participatory process. A strategy may describe the format, frequency, and location of consultations; a summary of the main issues raised and the views of participants; an account of the impact of consultations on design of the strategy; and a discussion of the role of civil society in future monitoring and implementation.

Reducing Debt Burdens

In 1996, the World Bank and the IMF unveiled the **HIPC Initiative** to reduce the debt burdens of the world's poorest countries. This initiative was viewed as a means of helping the countries concerned achieve economic growth and reduce poverty.

While a number of countries qualified for the initiative—and debt relief in nominal terms totaling more than $6 billion had been committed to seven countries by September 1999—concern grew that the initiative did not go far enough, or fast enough.

Consequently, when the new approach to poverty reduction was introduced in 1999, the initiative was enhanced to provide:

The savings from debt relief should be used for health, education, and other poverty-reducing social programs

- broader and deeper debt relief, through lower debt targets. For example, the number of countries eligible for debt relief under the enhanced HIPC Initiative is 38, compared with 29 formerly.
- faster debt relief, through financing at an earlier stage of the policy program to free up resources for poverty-reducing spending, such as on health and education.

Combined with debt relief outside the HIPC Initiative, countries are expected to see their debt stocks reduced on average by about two-thirds, freeing money for social spending.

As of July 2004, 27 low-income countries—23 in sub-Saharan Africa—had begun to receive debt relief under the HIPC Initiative.

The eligible countries are low-income countries that have unsustainable debt burdens; most are in Africa. For these countries, even full use of traditional mechanisms of debt rescheduling and debt reduction—together with aid, concessional loans, and the pursuit of sound policies—are not sufficient for them to reach a "sustainable" level of external debt, that is, a level of debt that can be serviced comfortably through export earnings, aid, and capital inflows, while maintaining an adequate level of imports.

Under the HIPC Initiative, debt reduction is provided to support policies that promote economic growth and poverty reduction. Part of the job of the IMF, working in collaboration with the World Bank, is to help ensure that the resources provided by debt reduction are not wasted: debt reduction alone, without the right policies, would bring no benefit in terms of poverty reduction. And policies to reduce poverty need to be supported not only by debt relief, but also by increased aid flows from the richer countries and by improved access for developing countries to industrial countries' markets.

Success in promoting broadly shared growth and, especially, helping to ensure that the poor are not left ever farther behind, is a collective responsibility of the entire international community. The IMF is striving to make its contribution, as part of its efforts to help ensure that globalization works for the benefit of all.

Children visit the IMF Center in Washington, D.C. The Center is open to the public, and has exhibits about the role of the IMF in the global economy